D1264070

TWO HEADS. 1959. Collage

JEAN ARP

By Jean Cathelin

Translated from the French by Enid York
Color Photographs by Luc Joubert

Seven Color Plates

Forty Black and White
Illustrations

GROVE PRESS, INC.   ·   NEW YORK
EVERGREEN BOOKS, LTD., LONDON

Distributed in Canada
by McClelland & Stewart Ltd.
25 Hollinger Road, Toronto 16

COPYRIGHT © 1959 BY GEORGE FALL, PARIS
First Grove Press Edition 1959
Library of Congress Catalog Card Number:
59-114403

Jean Arp is published in two editions:
      An Evergreen Gallery Book
      A cloth bound edition

Grove Press Books and Evergreen Books are
published by Barney Rosset at Grove Press, Inc.,
64 University Place, New York 3, N. Y.

Color Plates and Black and White Illustrations
printed in France

MANUFACTURED IN THE UNITED STATES OF AMERICA

When, at the age of ten, I heard the word spoken by my father and his surrealist friends, I did not at first believe that it was the name of a living being, but rather the magic symbol for some thing, in the special sense in which a pebble, a twig, or a cloud shaped like a horseman's head are *things*. This intuition was well founded, as I discovered when I was able to attend his exhibitions and to read the collected volumes of contemporary reviews. And further confirmation was given me when I heard Arp explain that his unique name was nothing more than the Germanization of the word Harpe, which had come about when his ancestors had passed from a French-speaking to a German-speaking land.

This turning of Harpe into Arp is a true rendering in linguistic terms of the artist's position as a person and of his work at that point where French rationalism hinges onto German romanticism—a place of privilege, and an unequaled window onto the world through which the two main streams of Western culture come to synthesize in his own person. This hinge position makes itself felt when expressed in the international language of plastic shapes no less than in the more fragmentary, more parochial language of verbal forms.

These two contrary elements set Arp's course toward a dialectical succession of cycles, and once his work had reached its full maturity, a constructive cycle was to follow a destructive one, a subjective phase to give place to an objective one. But throughout this evolution one permanent quality has persisted—spirituality, a brand of spirituality not linked with theosophy, like Mondrian's or Brancusi's, but rather a material sublimation, like Klee's. Both artists turn to matter in their search for the origin of the spirit, both bow to matter when they try to show their allegiance to the natural order of the world rather than to the order that man has superimposed upon it, whereas the Dutch *De Stijl* movement is superhumanist in spirit and tends to impose a more highly perfected human order. The spirituality of *De Stijl* is in some measure functional, it is an instrument of power, recognized and made use of as such; while in Klee or Arp spirituality is a natural upsurge, the mimesis of man in tune with the cosmos, a pantheistic assertion that the supremely reasonable course for man is to submit to the unreason of things.

This natural history begins on September 16, 1887, when Jean Arp was born at Strasbourg into an Alsatian family of mingled French and German roots.

It is not surprising, therefore, that from the age of fifteen, being thoroughly integrated in his own times—like most of those born under the sign of Virgo—he should feel drawn by the European spirit of *Der Stürmer* (the name of a group and of a review), whose leading exponent René Schickele, was a perfect example of Franco-German cultural fusion. There was less than five years age difference between them. The schoolboy admirer of Brentano's *Tales of the Rhine* and of the poems of Novalis could not but be at home in the company of Alsatians and Germans, none of whom had much use for the Prussian monarchy. Here he found also Anette Kolb, the expressionist poet Ernst Stadler (killed at the front in 1914), Flake and many others.

In 1904, Arp went to Paris alone for the first time, to stay with an uncle near La Motte-Picquet. What interested him most was modern painting. On his return to Strasbourg he entered the School of Applied Arts. A new review had succeeded *Der Stürmer,* again edited by René Schickele, *Das Neue Magazin*. A few of his poems appeared in it, and the following year, at eighteen, work of his was published through Karl Gruber, in *l'Anthologie de la Poésie Alsacienne Contemporaine*.

By now, painting and poetry had become inseparable for him. He set out for the School of Fine Arts in Weimar and only left the teach-

FLOWER-HAMMER. 1917. Painted wood. 24¾ x 19¾"
In two versions:
1. Collection F. Arp, Paris. 2. Collection of the artist

ing of von Hofman for a year's stay in Paris, where he attended classes at the Académie Julian. ✻

Well-equipped with the tools of his trade, he returned once more to Weggis in Switzerland, where his people were living. By this time he was reducing the Alpine landscape to an interplay of lines in his work. He was on the road to abstraction. His part in the first exhibition of *Moderne Bund* (Lucerne, 1911), along with Herbin, Matisse, and Picasso, brought him before the public eye. He corresponded with Kandinsky, went to see him in Munich, and joined the *Blaue Reiter* group.

From then on, he became one of the most active men in modern art. He met Robert Delaunay, wrote for *Der Sturm,* Herwarth Walden's review and the chief organ of the German expressionist movement, and showed his works in Berlin at the gallery with the same name.

Just before the war he became acquainted with Max Ernst in Cologne. In Paris, Delaunay and Max Jacob put him in touch with Picasso, Modigliani, Apollinaire, and all the noted men of his generation.

A resolute pacifist and a Frenchman at heart, he went to Switzerland in order not to have to fight on the German side. In 1915, Zurich became once and for all his second home, for it was there that he met a young woman painter who had come to see an exhibition of his first collages at the Tanner Gallery, Sophie Taeuber. Only her accidental death in 1943 was to part them.

This is not the place in which to write an historical account of Dada, founded the following year at the now famous Cabaret Voltaire in Zurich. From its inception, Arp and Sophie were in the forefront of its shock troops with Hugo Ball, Tristan Tzara, Richard Huelsenbeck and Marcel Janco. The collected numbers of the review *Dada,* and of *391,* Picabia's magazine, bear witness to Arp's activity, which continued until 1919, when, with Ernst, he founded a branch of Dada at Cologne. All its heroes have related with emotion their memories of this period. Recently Walter Mehring, in *La Bibliothèque Perdue* (Julliard, 1958), undertook to write a timely critical memoir.

Arp took part in all its activities and contributed to every issue of the magazine in the form of poems, woodcuts, and reproductions.

Arp was hard at work. Since 1917 he had given up collages and tapestry and begun to work on abstract wood reliefs. At this time too he was doing dual-paintings, either with his wife or with Ernst; anonymity had a great attraction for him; the search for the anonymity of cathedrals was soon to become an attempt to equal the anonymity of the natural phenomenon of erosion.

An important turning-point in his life occurred in 1925 when he left the German-Swiss world in favor of Paris. He took part in the surrealists' first exhibitions and demonstrations, and settled at Meudon in the pleasant house where he still lives, and which Sophie designed with prophetic genius. Here he brought forth the first of his wood or bronze reliefs which were the forerunners of those at the universities of Harvard and Caracas, and of the panel at the UNESCO Palace in Paris. Sophie Taeuber-Arp was commissioned to do the interior decoration of l'Aubette at Strasbourg, and asked Arp and Theo Van Doesburg to collaborate with her. The first high-reliefs were conceived for these walls, but unfortunately, due to the stupidity of a shopkeeper, nothing remains of them today but photographs. The Strasbourgers were to wait until Arp's seventieth birthday before they exhibited his works and made much of him, having been among the first to mock at his plastic creations.

In 1930, he discovered the plastic possibilities of torn paper, at the time his poems were being translated into French by the surrealists. He worked ceaselessly to be able to write his poems thereafter in French. About the same time, he stopped using wood in favor of plaster and marble. He took part in the creation of the *Abstraction-Création* movement, and before anyone else—through his work in the round—he showed the profound unity which exists between abstraction and surrealism, between the subjective subconscious and the objective pantheistic conscious. At this time too he published his first short works in French.

Since then he has lived a retired life wholly dedicated to his work. Sculptures, reliefs, poems, all are evidence of a full mastery of his art. His plastic work has become ever purer, reaching the essential and climbing the path toward spirituality until it has attained a kind of mystique of matter. At the same time the humor of his poems seeks to destroy the false anthropomorphic universe and helps to raise a barrier between the poet and that universe.

But this fruitful communion with nature was shattered by the war. Arp and Sophie took refuge at Grasse, where they met again Sonia Delaunay—Robert had just died at Montpellier, a few days before Allendy—and the Italian painter, Magnelli. When the Nazis invaded the Southern Zone, the Arps crossed into Switzerland. On January 13, 1943 a tragedy took place, the accidental death of Sophie in Zurich where they had met twenty-eight years earlier. Arp laid bare his grief in some harrowing poems.

After the Liberation, like all the creators of true modern art, the art that had been banned by those whose ideal had been to re-create the Middle Ages, Arp enjoyed a sudden popularity. He was recognized at last as an artist of the very front rank. Galleries the world over fought for his works, as did the great private collectors. From Paris to Berlin and New York, complete editions of his poems appeared everywhere, and the larger galleries organized retrospective exhibitions of his work. Arp went twice to America, and fled from Paris to Switzerland in order to work far from the growing crowds of art-lovers. The International Prize for Sculpture of the 1954 Venice Biennale marked the peak of an overwhelming wave of popularity.

This in brief is the life story of a smiling young man of seventy who, because of heart trouble, has had to give up his chisel and his carving and confine himself to modeling in plaster; now too with pencil, brush, and etching needle, he draws, paints, and cuts reliefs in his latest period of unmatched serenity, so well-balanced that the total discard of non-essentials has led not to aridity but to deep inner richness.

Let us now go on to study the evolution of his work, which appears to have all the simplicity of an object integrated in the world of nature, yet the very simplicity of which conceals complex workings like some mysterious poetic cauldron.

In the summer of 1915, when he went to Switzerland, Arp left behind him his early student works. At twenty-seven, he had already given up painting as such, being thwarted by its spatial flatness which forced him into abstraction, whereas his very concrete imagination had for long been seeking to express the sum total of the dimensions. He was to return to it again only occasionally, as a relaxation. And yet, upon his arrival in Zurich, his first act was to destroy the figurative and expressionist sculptures that he had executed between 1903

CLOCK. 1924. Painted wood. 26 x 22½″
Collection of the artist

and 1912 at different times during his stays at Weggis while he was learning to sculpt under Fritz Huf.

Therefore, of his work prior to 1915 there only remain the engravings and illustrations published in 1912 and 1913, notably in Kandinsky's *Blaue Reiter* publication. In these he carries expressionism to its peak, and his taste for the dreamlike and the haphazard begins to break through. His strokes are already entirely free; both as an illustrator and as an engraver he is practiced and faultless: all his life Arp has done an enormous amount of drawing, which is why he is able to extract every atom of significance from a flat stroke or from a curve in space. But the young artist is still very much influenced by the men he met in Paris, Switzerland, and Munich. He is still very close to Klee and Kandinsky, and in particular, he seems drawn toward abstraction in the same spirit as the latter, a logical outcome for a man who has reached the limit of expressionism.

But this is not taking into account Arp's humor, something very foreign to the grave author of *On the Spiritual in Art.* Arp is neither critic nor theorist. He is lucidly aware of artistic events and of their place in the world, but he cannot build up a system. Both his humor and his childlike naivety keep him from doing so. In this he is more closely allied to Klee than to Mondrian and Kandinsky.

He is the very reverse of the intellectual theorist; like a sensitive plate which records and interprets the movements of his time, this man, who is in direct communcation with that natural universe which lies hidden beneath the universe of man, transmits these movements, but the masses as yet are not receptive to the messages which press in upon him, and so he has the semblance of a forerunner and a prophet. This quirk of fortune appealed to both the poet and the humorist in him.

He was already deeply permeated by the spirit if not by the letter of Dada and surrealism, when in 1915 he wrote the poems *Chair de rêve.* Along with some brilliantly devised images and the first sparks of a new humor of which he, with Picabia, Tzara, and later Crevel, was to be the grand creator, *(autour des alouettes spongieuses pullule le ciel rocailleux—les bateaux basculent dans leurs fauteuils à bascule —les morts se réveillent sous leurs globes),*[1] he expresses the disquiet

[1]around the spongy larks the rocky sky swarms—the boats are rocking in their rocking-chairs—the dead awaken beneath their glass cases. (*Trans.*)

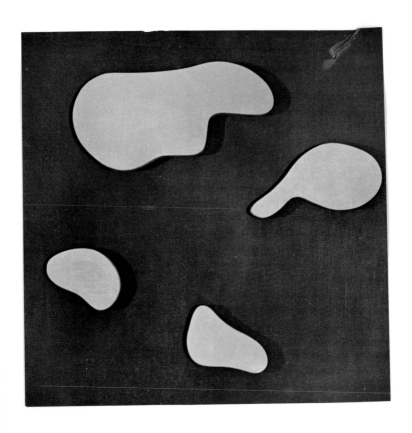

MEETING. 1934. Wood and oil. 26 x 26″
Collection of the artist

and the revolutionary spirit of his generation. *(les portes du monde s'ouvrent et se ferment avec fracas—le temps se transforme en poupée de cire—san arrêt le surnéant tire sur l'oeuf de l'harmonie).*[1] Here he defines his esthetics for the first time and puts into words his great idea of the domination of nature over the animal and human world. *(les arbes se font leurs oiseaux sur mesure).*[2]

The time was not far off when he was to pass on to the total emancipation of language and imagery, though in a less mechanical way than the Italian futurists, making use of childish puns and English nonsense of the nursery rhyme and limerick kind. *(pas par pas sont des pas sans pas* or *le bleu veut happer le bleu).*[3] Robert Minder, professor of German Literature at the Sorbonne, has not been afraid to say that these plays on sound, this treatment of the word as something whose roots and functions can be cut and distorted, are as reminiscent in their linguistic behavior of his contemporary Martin Heidegger as of the medleys of the Middle Ages.

At the same time he was impelled toward the de-mystification of the plastic arts as well as of language. Much later he was to find his own brand of myth and mystery, but first of all he had to make a clean sweep of an art accepted by all but unacceptable to him, because it had no bearing on the cosmos, an art reduced to a purely decorative function, an art for boudoirs and courtesans. He was to write in 1933, in *Les Cahiers d'art,* an article whose title alone perfectly explains and justifies his revolt: *"Le style éléphant contre le style bidet."*

When he met Sophie in 1915 he was helping, by means of his collages and tapestries, in the cubist demolition work, using the process which later on André Breton happily named *"Le détournement de fond"* (Fundamental Reorientation).[4] He re-naturalized objects which had lost all meaning through our conventions and society's false sense of what is sacred. But whereas the cubists respect the in-

---

[1]the doors of the world open and shut with a crash—time turns into a wax doll —ceaselessly Supernothingness shoots at the egg of harmony.

[2]trees have their birds made to measure.

[3]step by step is a stepless step *or* blue wants to grip blue.

[4]A pun which sounds like "misappropriation of funds." (*Trans.*)

1. TORSO. 1931. White marble. 24 x 15½ x 7″. Collection Müller Widmann, Basel.
2. BUDS. 1938. Original plaster. 16 x 7½ x 8″.
3. LUNAR BREASTPLATE. 1938. Pink limestone. 12½ x 14½″. Winston Collection, Birmingham (Mich.).
4. GEOMETRIC-AGEOMETRIC. 1942. Bronze. 11½ x 11 x 6″.
5. THE MERMAID. 1942. Bronze. 17½ x 13 x 9″.
6. SCULPTURE OF SILENCE, "THE CROW." 1942. Pink limestone. 19½ x 21½ x 17½″. Galleria d'Arte Moderna, Turin.
7. BIRD SKELETON. 1947. Bronze. 15 x 8 x 8″.
8. & 9. DREAM ANIMAL. 1947. Bronze. 15 x 8 x 8″.
10. BUST OF ELF. 1949. Bronze. 12 x 5½ x 4″.
11. HEAD ON CLAWS. 1949. Bronze. 18 x 9 x 7½″.
12. CONCRETE SCULPTURE, "MIRR." 1949-1950. Black granite. 13 x 14½ x 19″. Collection H. de Rothschild, New York.
13. EVOCATION OF A SPECTRAL LUNAR HUMAN FORM. 1950. Marble variant with small plinth. 36 x 25½ x 19½″. Collection Dotremont, Brussels.
14. EVOCATION OF A SPECTRAL LUNAR HUMAN FORM. 1950. White marble on plinth. 36 x 25½ x 19½″. Collection Dotremont, Brussels.
15. SMALL MYTHICAL FIGURE. 1950. Original plaster. 37½ x 6 x 7″.
16. MYTHICAL FIGURE. 1950. Original plaster. 44 x 15 x 13½″. Collection Zervos, Paris.
17. IDOL. 1950. Plaster. 42½ x 15 x 8″.
18. THALES OF MILETUS. 1951. Black granite. 41 x 9 x 10½″. Collection G. David Thompson, Pittsburgh.
19. CYPRIAN SCULPTURE. 1951. White marble. 15½ x 22 x 12½″. Private collection, U.S.A.
20. COBRA-CENTAUR. 1952. White marble. 30½ x 16½ x 9″. Musée des Beaux-Arts, Wintherthur (Switzerland).
21. EXCESSES OF A MYTHOLOGICAL WINESKIN (Outrance d'une Outre Mythique). 1952. Pink limestone. 13½ x 19½ x 18″. Art Institute of Chicago.
22. TORSO. 1953. White marble. 34 x 13 x 10½″. Museum of Smith College, Northampton (Mass.).

23. & 24. AQUATIC. 1953. White marble. 9 x 13½ x 25″. Walker Art Center, Minneapolis (Minn.).

25. EARLY FOREBEAR. 1953. Wood. 9 x 3 x 3½″. Collection M. Hagenbach, Basel.

26. PTOLEMY. 1953. Hauteville stone. 40 x 20½ x 16½″. Collection Burden, New York.

27. DREAM FLOWER WITH SNOUT. 1954. Marble on plinth. 31 x 10½ x 7″. Collection Mrs. H. Gates Lloyd, Washington.

28. AGONIZING CONFIGURATION. 1955. Limestone. 11½ x 7 x 5½″.

29. CHOSEN BY THE FLOWERS. 1957. Bronze. 10½ x 10½ x 8½″.

30. & 31. KOREAN TORSO. 1958. White marble. 38 x 4½ x 6″.

32. PLATE WITH NAVEL AND FORKS. 1923. Paint on cardboard. 23 x 24″. Sidney Janis Gallery, New York.

33. HEAD WITH MUSTACHE. MUSTACHES AND MASK. 1930. Paint on wood. 33 x 43″.

34. CONSTELLATION. 1932. Paint on wood. 27 x 33″. Collection Felix Witzinger, Basel.

35. PREADAMITE FIGURE. 1952. Wood. 8 x 10″.

36. DANCER II. 1955 (from a 1923 relief). Oil on canvas. 56 x 43″. Collection François Arp, Paris.

37. HEAD-BOTTLE. 1956 (from a 1928 drawing). Painted pavatex. 51 x 33″.

38. THE TWINS. 1956 (from a 1929 drawing). Painted pavatex. 32 x 22½″.

39. SKELETON AND MUSTACHE. 1956 (from a 1927 drawing). 39 x 29″. Collection C. Cardazzo, Milan.

40. AWAKENING. 1957 (in memory of a 1923 embroidery). Relief in painted pavatex. 27 x 26″.

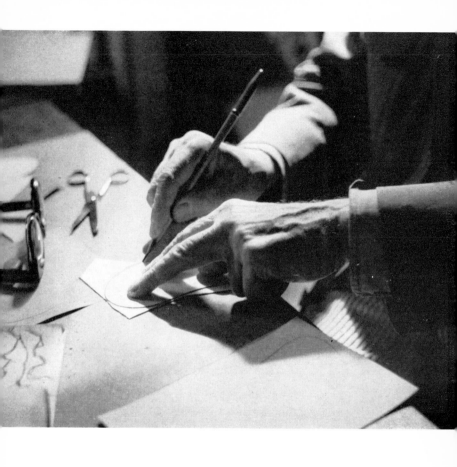

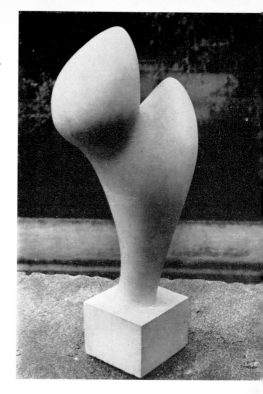

◀ 4

5
▼

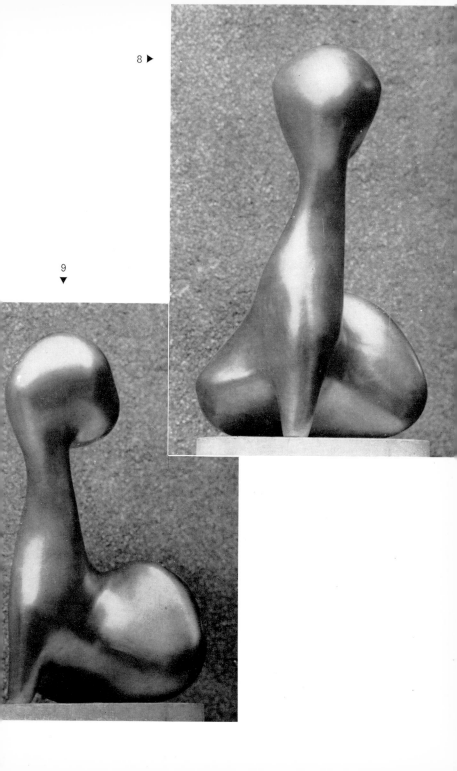

8 ▶

9
▼

10 ▶

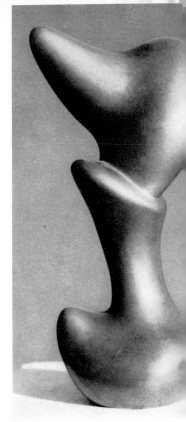

11
▼

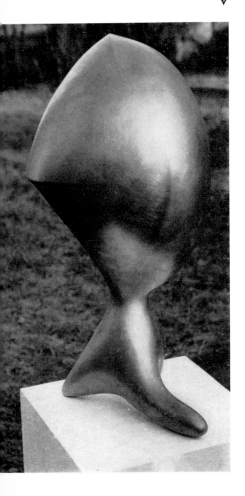

13 ▶

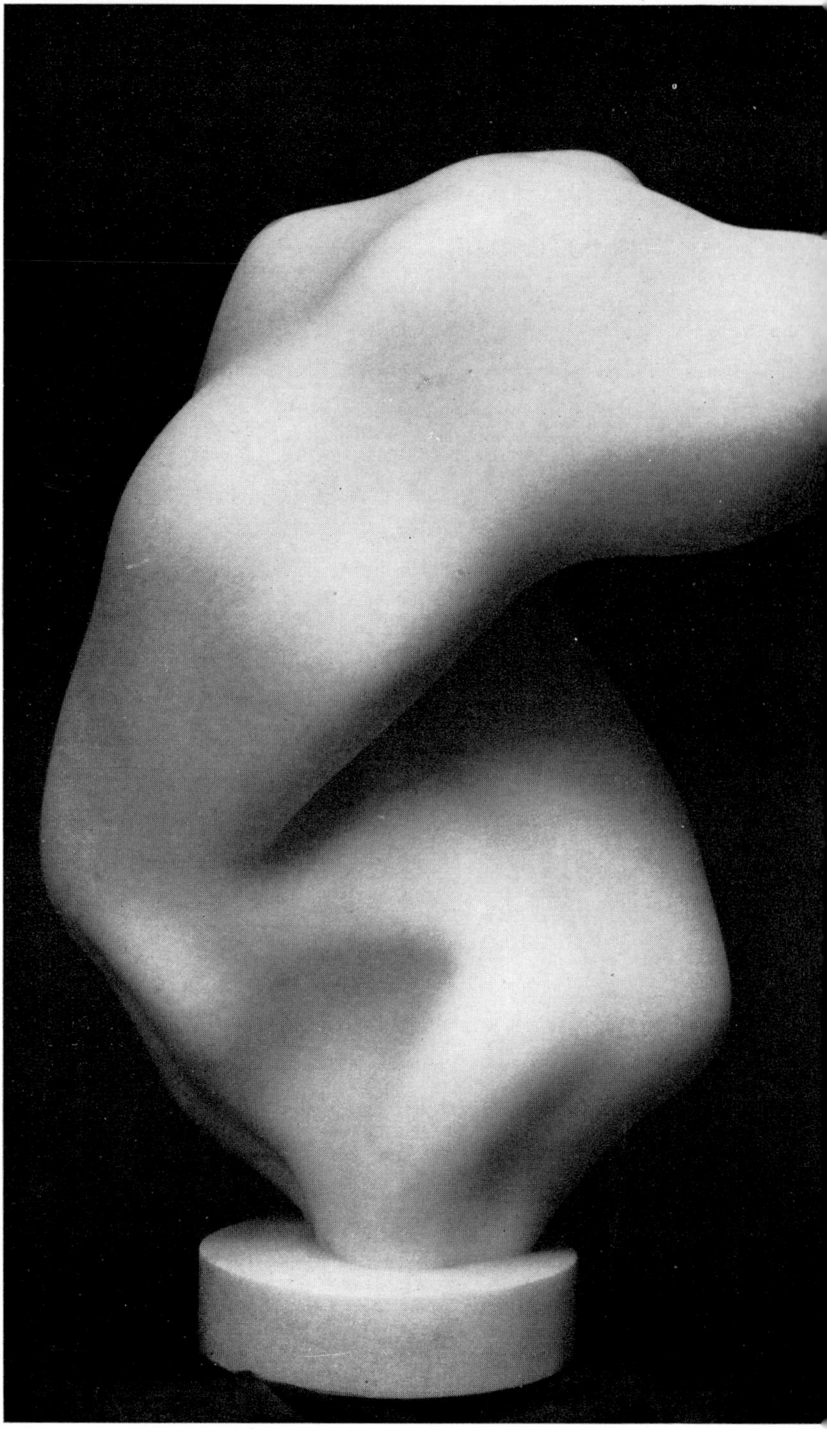

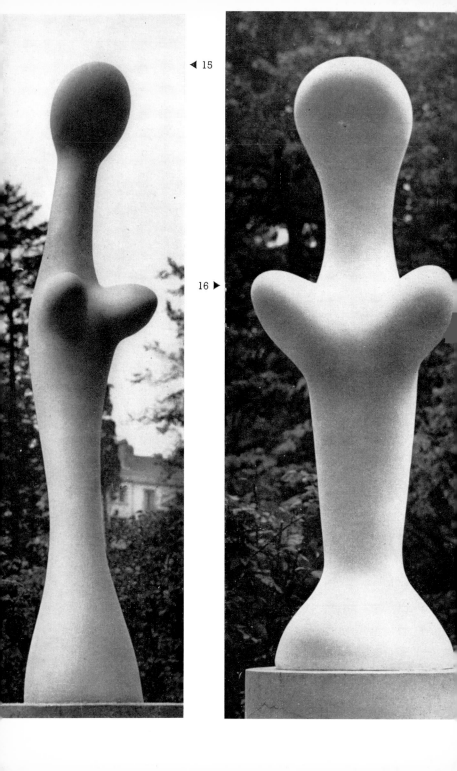

◀ 15

16 ▶

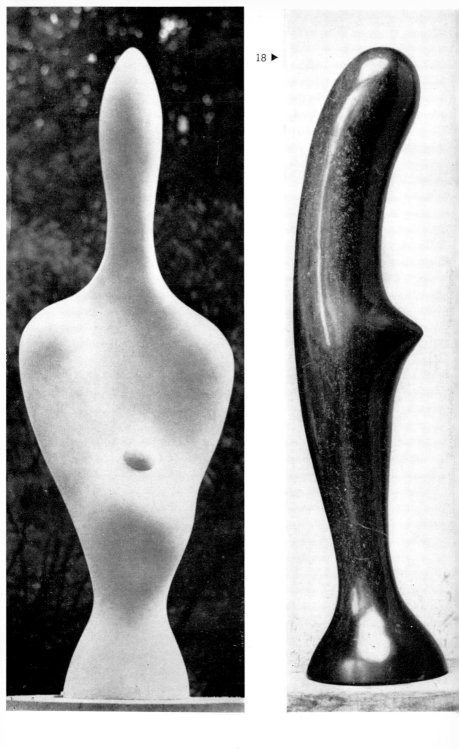

18 ▶

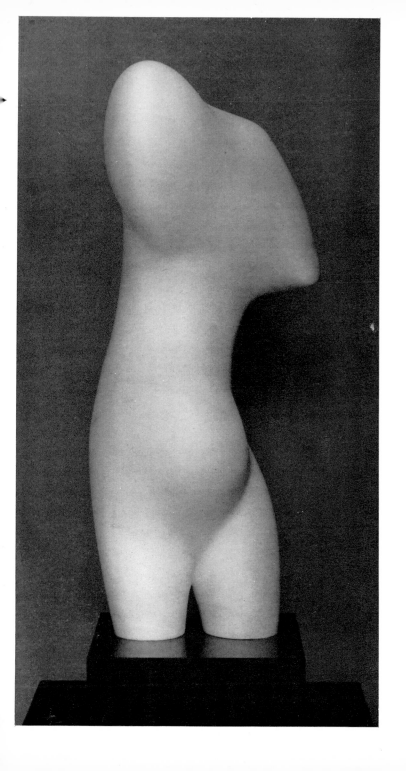

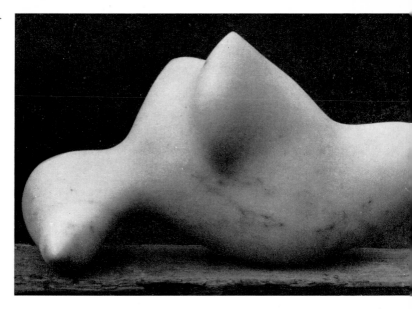

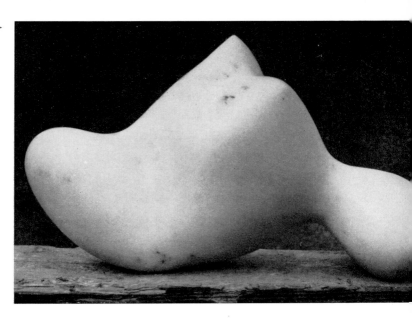

25
▼

26 ▶

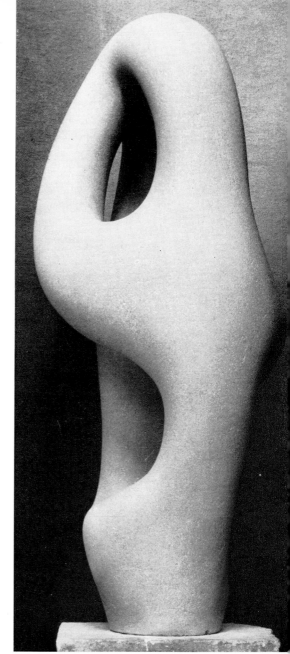

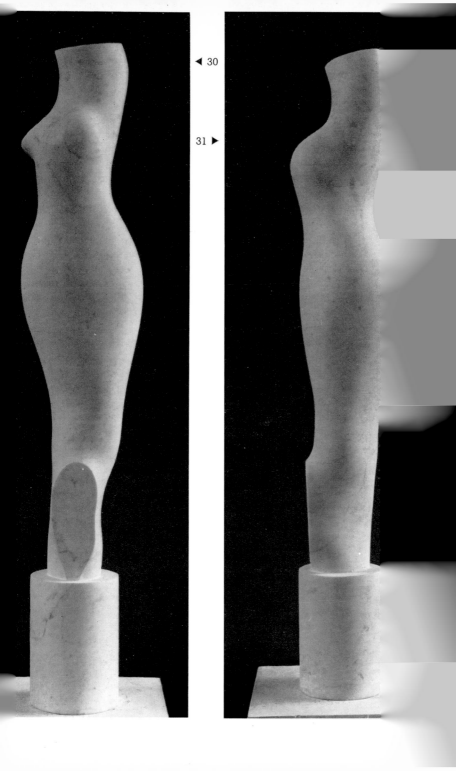

◄ 30

31 ►

◀ 36

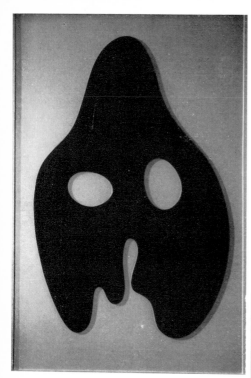

◄ 37

38
▼

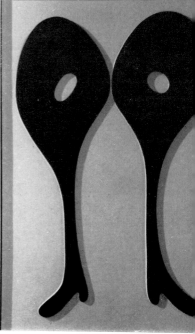

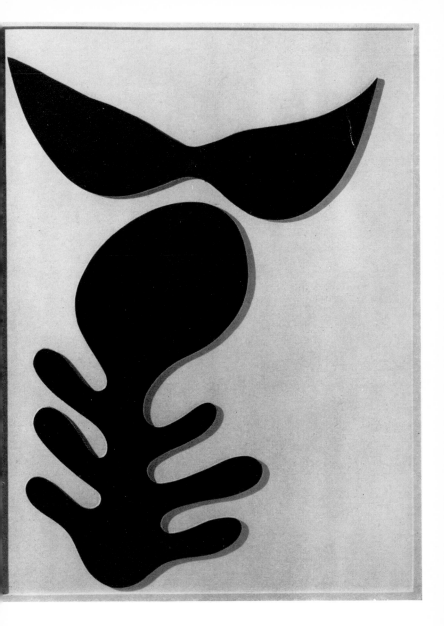

tegral nature of an object, when they paint shattered billiard balls, or bits of newspaper on the hull of a ship, Arp makes great scissor cuts into the living tissue of his subject. In his collages, shreds of material, bits of pasteboard, and scraps of paper lose their identity to find themselves again as fragments of a natural product and given a new meaning by the mere ordering of the composition, partly according to the whim of chance, partly according to the artist's will, thus establishing from the outset of the work that wonderfully compelling duality of the conscious-unconscious.

But Sophie was painting, and her work, already completely abstract, had the same spirit as that of Delaunay in Paris, the constructivists in Moscow, and the suprematists of Malevitch's group in Poland. Michel Seuphor most justly says of it in his *Dictionary of Abstract Painting:* "It is neoplasticism before its time." Indeed, the artists of the Dada movement were not to know the *De Stijl* group until much later. From the fact of their life together, Arp and Sophie influenced each other. Together they attempted to create an "absolute" art, painting certain works jointly. Their line-play in two dimensions is akin to the work being done at that time by Malevitch and Magnelli. Yet all three were as yet unaware of one another, which indicates both the profound necessity today for abstract art, and also the general unity of the human spirit at that period, at all events among artists who sought to repudiate the anthropomorphic world that was crumbling to ruins amid the fearful butchery of war. Purity of line and color was sought not only for its own sake, but also as expression of a need for spiritual uplift and a wish to establish a great world order above the false and sentimental national order.

Soon, however, Arp found these pursuits leading him toward aridity; geometrism drove him up against a wall. This striving for the absolute, he confessed to me one day recently at Meudon, suddenly appeared to him to lead to the brink of madness, to end in the impossible masterpiece and total nothingness. Only a man like Malevitch would go to the length of a square monochrome. While Sophie was working it out of her system by introducing a musical rhythm with preoccupations similar to those of Robert and Sonia Delaunay, Arp was throwing himself into chance arrangement.

The organized unreason of Dadaism was to be the safety-valve against the snares of the reasonable. At first Arp repudiated wise, dangerous geometry by cutting out and sticking on—"following the laws of chance" (which is the title of a 1916 work)—those neat little squares which others contrive to arrange within the limit of the mathematical and the metaphysical.

Suddenly dream shapes, phantoms, shades of mustaches or of clocks began to sprawl over the white pages of avant-garde reviews in great flat blacks. Arp seized upon a means of expression and made it entirely new: the woodcut.

May I venture to suggest a possible explanation? Arp had long felt a need for sculpture, but he had destroyed his first carvings and had not yet found his form of expression in this medium. On the other hand, he was no longer satisfied with painting, and its freer substitute, collage, was still too flat for him. The reviews had little money behind them and those of his friends who contributed to their somewhat spasmodic publication or compilations of poems could not afford expensive line or half-tone photogravure plates. Against the metal plate used for the reproduction of official works or for the circulation of news photographs, Arp re-established the manual importance of the oldest of all methods of typographical reproduction: the woodcut.

And on the printed page, these woodcuts were to take on such autonomy, to shed so completely their modest role as mere illustration, to become to so high a degree a means of expression in their own right, that Arp came, unconsciously I believe, to feel that the woodcut is not only a means of reproduction. That, I imagine, is how Arp's woodcuts came to leave the printed page and hang on the wall. Why pull off copies from a woodcut, when the woodcut itself is an object capable of dethroning the painted picture from its royal supremacy? And why not borrow color from painting when it appears necessary? And in this way, Arp's invention, sometimes polychrome, sometimes monochrome, broke upon the world, this hitherto unknown "relief," halfway between sculpture and painting, an invention which is due—I suggest on the authority of Arp himself—to the frustration of a practiced engraver who found that printing from woodcuts deprived him of space and flattened his planes.

That is why it is impossible to exaggerate the historical importance of a work such as *Flower-Hammer,* in wood and six colors (including white), executed in 1916. Air circulates freely between the super-

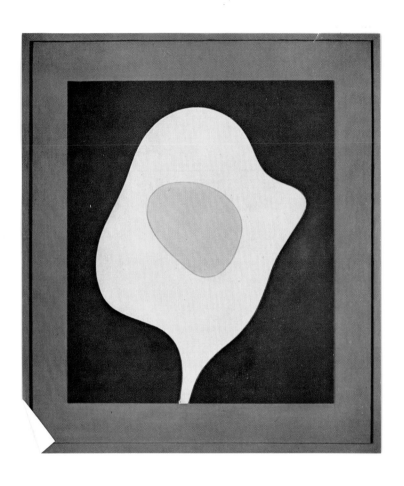

PROFILE. 1955. Oil on board. 27 x 24¼"
Collection of the artist

imposed planes, the picture leaps into space, the frame is a thing of the past. In *Configuration, Terrestrial Forms,* and other works of the same period, all reference to things seen disappears, but not all reference to nature. For Arp discovered a great truth: since his mind, in deep communion with matter, cannot be satisfied by the extrapolation of cosmic shapes resulting from his recourse to the geometric element, another way of escape from vulgar, photographic art opened to him. He now strove to convey inorganic shapes, shapes expressing telluric forces, the continual movement and gestation of the planet, and of the universe in which it takes its place. Where the traditional artist saw only those ordered shapes, logically associated with our domesticating and anthropomorphic sense of vision—a tree or a forest—Arp was to substitute a *subterraneous* reality, which cannot be perceived, but only felt or sensed.

And so he rediscovered primitive totemic art, an art that expresses shape in a state of flux that cannot be halted. He re-stated the prime importance of the elementary graphic symbol. Whereas the cubists were passionate defenders of the distortion of the human face, as practiced in Negro art, Arp, turning away from the expressionism which he once practiced, drew nearer to the Japanese or Indian idiom, and, by means of hitherto unknown, unperceived forms, revealed himself to be the forerunner of the formless.

The spirit of Dada brought to his work another dimension. Having reached the point of being able to express the essential by stripping his work bare, he was now able to afford the luxury of creating a new form of caricature. In a spirit of fun at first, but soon with a certain gravity breaking through, he fashioned his wood into the mutilated shapes of everyday things. In an entirely new vein, he recorded the destructive stamp of time on familiar objects, he manufactured objects dug up from the past (*Mask,* 1918) as he was to do later in sculpture, and he attacked and ridiculed those instruments by means of which we think to gain mastery over time and space (*Clock,* 1924). He reduced man to the humble place which is in fact his in the order of things; to this step we owe the *Torsos* reduced to their simplest expression, the humanoid ovoids, a whole weird bestiary in which a strange near-physical animal soon figured prominently, now negative, now positive, the mustache. In this Dadaistic urge to demolish, there is something of Alfred Jarry and of

Lewis Carroll. That is to say that in his humor, cruelty is always tempered by a breath of fairyland. Nothing is spared; *Shirtfronts, Forks,* and many other objects are made unreal and reduced to their simplest expression—and are all the more expressive for it, like a word judiciously substituted for another in controlled paraphasia. This art, to all appearance simple and easy, yet disturbing to fools, peoples the world with untamed monsters in which we are quick to recognize many things we had fondly imagined to be domesticated through and through, and which we suddenly find have turned against us, rebelling against our sway.

His genius coming into its own, and also as a proof that his aim had been true and that at last this too submissive world was becoming unbearable, he launched forth into *Shirts with Navel,* and those straggling designs like bits of string aping our deceitful handwriting. They hang on the walls of galleries and universities, locked up as a safeguard against their spreading through the streets, and as if, too, they could be set up as amulets *a contrario* against the revolt of things, when in fact they are statements of the triumphant revolt of man in his attempt to regain his place as "object of the first instance" in the concert of the universe.

They slipped unchecked into the world of efficiency and daily life. All over the globe, cafés, shops, and places of entertainment are sloughing off their skins to take on a new decoration inspired by the two most significantly free artists of the age, Arp and Miró, who often perpetrated their solemn jokes together. Their clouds, their figures now conceal the neon tubes which we no longer wish to see. Better still, Arp's navels, his funny men, and ovoid constellations have settled down and are very much at ease in the world of our children, difficult as it is to enter: the most modern toys, called "functional," whose nonfigurative and imprecise shapes fit into each other according to the chance of childish whims, seem to derive straight from the "Arpiad."

Arp has never stopped creating wood reliefs, but they became rarer after 1930 during his great period of sculpture. They reappeared as his chief medium of expression after 1954 when the state of his health forbade him to practice the true work of a sculptor, carving, and allowed him only to model in plaster.

Arp's return to sculpture in 1930 constitutes both a crucial moment in his work as a whole and an important stage in the history of modern art. In groping through reliefs, collages, painting and torn paper work, he had fashioned for himself an inimitable style, though often imitated, and above all, he had found the road he sought. He had only abandoned true sculpture because he did not feel ready to set his seal upon it. When he took up the chisel once again, or when he decided to model in plaster with a view to bronze casting, it was as an artist of forty-three in full possession of his talents, who knew perfectly well where he was going.

That is why the new shapes he gave to marble and to metal very soon compelled recognition and placed him in the front rank of great contemporary sculptors.

But it must be emphasized that there is no break in his work as a whole. His sculptures in the round are the natural sequel to his reliefs. He now gives an autonomous place in nature to shapes which he had brought to life on the wall.

If he still asserts the presence of a subjacent world in our midst, he no longer merely sketches it in an agreeable, even sometimes in a decorative way. Henceforth he thrusts his way of seeing upon us.

This development is a continuation and not in any sense a disavowal. The last great reliefs of the 1925 period were veering toward sculpture, and after 1928, large works in cut-out wood appear, escaping from the frame and from the mural limitation of relief, and invading the circumambient air.

From the start his work in the round differs from the reliefs through a certain gravity—which does not exclude humor—and through a sense of the monumental. The reliefs always had until then, whatever their size, some semblance of the small and the pretty, the quality of something to be cherished. The sculptures, on the other hand, looming up in a world where danger threatens on every hand, assert themselves immediately as protectors.

So it is with the series of *Torsos* (1930-1931), in which flowing movement can be contrasted, in plastic terms, with the fixed movement of the reliefs. The curve of a buttock, of a belly, of shoulders which, detached from their arms, become mother-stones, are also metaphysical tokens. The work of man, mutilated, is united again with nature. And it will become the aim of sculpture, by destroying the rational formalism of work in the round, to achieve fusion be-

UNDER THE BLACK SUN OF JOY. 1958
Relief, painted board. 26¼ x 20¼″. Private collection

tween man's handiwork and nature, the artist setting himself up as demiurge inasmuch as he himself creates both the patina and the ravages of time. And, once naturalized, his marble, plaster, bronze, granite and basalt take on an air of protest: man is one with the cosmos, but he does not lose his identity, save by his smiling humility.

The reason for this permanence is that the disembodied spirit has been set aside as of less worth than the being of flesh and blood. These sculptures, even more than the reliefs, disclose the depths to which Arp's quest is directed on the purely human plane. The mystical fusion with the cosmos that he demands is not in any way a vague dream or a philosophical affectation. His logos could not be clearer: mind and matter are one—*matter is endowed with energy* is the key-definition of the Einstein era—one is born of the other, they are indissoluble. Beneath the chisel, movement is born of the ideas inspired by the original shape and veining of the block of stone; but then the interplay of curves thus conceived imparts to the rough stone a meaning which goes beyond the stone, yet remains faithful to the inspiration first derived from the raw material. *Thought is formed in the mouth,* wrote Tristan Tzara: here it is formed in stone.

Moreover, the primordial means of fusion between mind and matter now bursts triumphantly from his sculptures: sexuality. Sensual and sensitive, but never sentimental, Arp's sculptures evoke every aspect of the flesh, and of love, its natural flowering. From the marble *Torsos* which evoke the very essence of womanhood—tender, ardent, voluptuous—to bronzes such as *Sculpture to be shown in the woods* and *Head with Objects*—both works in which adventitious particles are simply placed upon a central body, like young oysters upon a mother oyster—his whole art conjures up gestation, birth, maturity and death. At every stage, all is threatened, all may not be, may never see the light of day: here is a life that springs from a narrow space at the very verge of nothingness, to declare itself a sensitive creative intelligence, beyond the laws of rational thought. Certainly never before has pantheism been carried so far toward its ultimate consequences; here it is removed from its romantic atmosphere of yesterday and assumes the pre-Hellenic classical spirit of Sumer and Mycene.

But if the full story of Arp's sculpture be needed, it will not be found merely in the study of his inmost message, or of his metaphysical kinships and their mystical link with his poetry.

Account must be taken too of the language of sculpture pure and simple, over and above any intention of its author, over and above all the philosophical small-change contributed by the viewer.

Which means that, however sure in its general lines Arp's work may be, the overall direction in which it carries us along and sustains us must be ascribed to his own history and to that of sculpture today.

His own story follows a clear but tortuous course. This may be taken to mean that, having reached the elementary in his last reliefs before his great period of sculptural creation, and having from the very first touched the elemental in his sculpture, Arp has progressively restored, from 1930 to 1939, a certain complexity to his works. Once having captured the simple shapes of subjacent nature, once sure of his bent, he was not unnaturally seized with joy of the virtuoso. It could be said with some truth that he passed from the relative simplicity of line of the concerto to all the symphony's complexity of interwoven themes.

And so we see the extreme simplicity and the supra-natural quality of *Moon Fruit* or *Giant Seed* succeeded by the interplay of planes in space from 1936 on, as in *Mirr* and certain of the *Shells*. And then in 1938 a new bestiary made its appearance, as if he were now anxious to people with living beings a universe hitherto composed solely of great masses of rock, living things which seem moreover to be both the offspring of the loves of these great shapes for each other, and also the descendants of the naturalized objects portrayed in the reliefs. And through it all, it is manifest that Arp has been true to the inner voice of nature which places him far apart from those virtuosos of sculpture whose heads are filled with the cerebral acrobatics of the post-cubists. The way all these forms blend with the landscape— where they are a hundred times more at home than in houses—is highly significant. Michel Seuphor tells in his *Mondrian* how, one day at Arp's house at Meudon, the great Dutch painter declared that he had a horror of trees. It can be imagined how Arp must have shuddered at this remark which to him, the man of the torso-trunks, was utter sacrilege!

While the "navel" and the interplay of planes make their appearance in large works like *Cyprian Sculpture* (sketched in 1931, executed in small size in 1938, and full size in 1951), in which proto-

Mediterranean inspiration is already discernible, at the same time he was producing *Small Reclining Figure* and *Lunar Breastplate.*

In 1941, a very fertile period, and until 1947, these "figures" often took precedence over the great earthy mass of *Concretions.* To these years belong *The Leaf,* and the *Mediterranean Group,* the barbaric slenderness of the latter being a reply to the great classical, Olympian assertion of *Orphic Dream* of the same period. With humor, and very conscious of being pulled this way and that by his taste for the grandiose on the one hand and his Germanic memories of gnomes on the other, Arp wittily mingles the two tendencies in *Geometric-Ageometric,* in which the "subject" is reminiscent of a figure, while the "plinth" belongs to the nature element.

In a recent poem, Arp clearly admits to a sharp consciousness of his art, and signifies also that he can see no shame in indulging in a love of "doing," of doing well, in a virtuosity which is not gratuitous and purely technical, but is like that of a child who has found a "good knack" for climbing a tree or a wall more easily.

> Where is my knife?
> I want to peel
> one of my subjects,
> so as to limber up,
> so as to get my hand in.

Thus, when he is not launching into grandiose works, the author of *Homage to Rodin* (a moving work in granite, 1938) knows that his chisel must be allowed to smile, must be given its head and left free to loose its phantasms upon the world. From *Somersault* to *Siren* (in this delicious little figure, the tail recalls the naturalized anchor of the reliefs) this tendency culminates in *Dream Animal* (1947). The precious aspect and the delicate, dreamlike look of these "figures" disappear in the later ones, which by their allegorical and mythical grandeur come closer to the monumental character of *Goblets, Concretions,* and *Shells.*

Indeed, from 1947-1950 on, the outrageous gnomes disappear. The *Skeleton of a Bird,* so full of movement, is succeeded by hieratic shapes.

On the far side of virtuosity and fantasy, Arp rediscovers his in-inermost voice, but now a majestic solidity and an elegant fullness

CONFIGURATION "SAILBOAT IN THE FOREST". 1958
Relief, painted board. 24½ x 21½". Galerie Edouard Loeb, Paris

take the place of the genetic heaviness of the first great planetary masses.

The synthesis of these two trends was becoming more and more complete. Already in 1942, the *Sculpture of Silence* (called *The Crow*) foreshadows his mythical rendering of movement, his way of fixing flight by means of eternal coordinates which transcend the common coordinates of time and space. But at the same time his romantic passion for movement remains. By a supreme effort of self-mastery, it seems, the artist sets himself to seize, from between two shapes of mythological stillness, a movement, or merely a threat of movement, as of something about to overbalance (*Superimposed Goblets*), to fix it, to place it in a state of permanent "stasis," as the writers of science-fiction might say. Thus the human torso no longer has the rigor of a centuries-old fossil it had in 1930, but is taken unaware in a kind of nocturnal struggle which includes a sense of the sexual (*Evocation of a Spectral Lunar Human Form*).

But these are exceptions among his latest works. For the last ten years, Arp seems to have indicated that the domain of great sculpture was essentially a monumental immobility, the intangible part of the myth. The Mediterranean light absorbed during his journeys in Greece and his stay at Grasse during the Occupation seems to have brought to the surface the solar side of him. Geodesic expressionism and the formlessness of Hades have given place to the midsummer fullness of Demeter. It is remarkable that the greatest specialists of this century in Hellenic art and civilization have, without a doubt, been the German-educated researchers of Arp's generation.

The reliefs, *Mediterranean Initial* and *Memory of Athens,* which mark the first full introduction of bronze and marble into the reliefs, are more than an avowal, they are a clear-cut statement of Arp's final lesson: with the forms of Mother-Earth as his point of departure, he takes his place today in the proto-historical lineage of Mediterranean sculpture, with *Idol, Mythical Figure, Thales of Milet, Cobra-Centaur* in 1950-1951. In 1953 and 1955, forsaking such grand themes, he returns to the sensuality of his first torsos to give us that manatee from another world, that sea-horse from beyond the skies which he calls *Aquatic,* and which suggests a lost figure stretching out its breast-arms to embrace the birth of the universe. To 1953 also belongs *Ptolemy,* in which for the first time air circulates between the curves, and the filled-in space gives place to the hollow, creating movement in repose. Here the symbol of a thought is made profoundly alive, caught in flight as in a snapshot. Last comes the starkness of *Daphne,* in which human trunk and tree-trunk unite as if to herald forever the dawn of time; not because Arp is a prophet of history's repetition, but rather because, when all is said and done, at the level where his work stands, history is null and void, and has no reason to be taken into consideration. At that level, man's vain agitations are no longer visible to the naked eye. All that remains to bear witness in our favor is art, and with it the things that give rise to its creation, the underlying, foetal part of ourselves, together with our constant cry to the stars from the depths of the earth. Here a certain harmony reigns, with which town-dwellers are seldom familiar, which is the contrary of the social order but in conformity with that of the universe, the innermost order of created things.

Finally the Heraclitean flux and the *Theos agenetos,* the still unborn God of Thales, are the answer to the great Dadaist jest. Dada was truly and totally achieved in Arp: the systematic destruction of the man-made world leads us to recognize unconditionally the complete independence of the cosmos from our makeshift organizations. Arp's metaphysic, though it has no formulated creed, suggests, by means of shapes and poems, that only those will be saved from utter emptiness who can rediscover the umbilical cord joining us to the earth and to the great outer space.

In this Arp is a forerunner of the twenty-first century. One day he will be recognized as the herald of an interplanetary art through which, renouncing all pride, our descendants will find their place in the scheme of existing or latent things, in this galaxy as in others. Within the framework of this magnificent humility, Arp's navels, his gestative shapes will be symbols as significant as the three hairs by which Buddha summons his disciples to the call of the Infinite, that paradise which is Nature perceived in its totality. Arp more than anyone else has tried to communicate this vision.

In this selected bio-bibliography, only some of the works, articles, and gallery catalogues concerning Jean Arp will be given, as his total bibliography is considerable.

It should be noted that the only attempt to catalogue his sculptures, followed by an almost complete catalogue of the works written about him and the publications to which he has contributed as an illustrator or author of poems and articles, was drawn up by Marguerite Hagenbach as an appendix to the last published work on Arp: *Jean Arp* by Carola Giedion-Welcker (Harry N. Abrams, Inc., New York, 1957, and Gerd Hatje, Stuttgart). This work includes a short twenty-page study of his work and a collection of black and white photographs of his reliefs and sculptures.

At the time of this writing, four important events connected with Arp have recently taken place:

1. Exhibition of twenty-one pieces at the Galerie d'Art Moderne in Basel (December 14, 1956-January 16, 1957).

2. Exhibition in Strasbourg, April-May, 1957. At the same time, in the publication *Allemagne d'Aujourd'hui,* the sixth number of which is devoted to the Alsatian School of literature and art, Professor Robert Minder, of the Sorbonne, celebrates Arp's 70th birthday by drawing a parallel between his language as poet and humorist, and the language of Martin Heidegger.

3. The opening of the Unesco Palace in the Place Fontenoy, Paris; along with Pablo Picasso, Henry Moore, and Joan Miró, Arp contributed to it with a copper relief 15 metres long.

4. A retrospective exhibition of reliefs, drawings, sculptures in the autumn of 1958 at The Museum of Modern Art in New York.

The first number, June 1958, of the review *Panderma,* at Basel, partly devoted to Arp's 70th birthday which was celebrated by his Dada friends, especially Richard Huelsenbeck.

Catalogues and Reviews

Les Feuilles Libres, No. 27 (1928). Contains ten woodcuts and text by Tzara.

Manomètre (Lyon, 1922-1932), a review published by Emile Malespine, psychiatrist and painter. Several numbers published woodcuts and poems in German by Arp.

Derrière le Miroir, No. 33 (1950). Catalogue of the exhibition at Galerie Maeght (45 sculptures, 14 reliefs, paintings, torn paper designs, collages, drawings). This catalogue contains six unpublished poems by Arp, a preface by P.-G. Bruguière and another by Jean Cathelin.

Catalogue of the exhibition at the Buchholz Gallery (Curt Valentin), January-February 1949. Preface by Jean Cathelin, short text by Arp, 15 reproductions and original cover. The exhibition contained 27 sculptures and reliefs and 18 collages.

Catalogue of the retrospective exhibition of collages shown at the Galerie Berggruen. A note by Arp giving historical account of the collages since 1914. A critical note on the exhibition by Léon Degand is to be found in *Aujourd'hui,* No. 6, January 1956.

Second Salon de la Sculpture Abstraite (Galerie Denise René, April-May 1956), ten sculptors including Arp. The text of the invitation by Jean Cathelin. On this occasion, Galerie Denise René published, in conjunction with *Aujourd'hui,* a 50-page album with texts and black and white illustrations, *Témoignages pour la Sculpture Abstraite.* Introduced by the poet and critic Pierre Guéguen, this album contains a brief article by Arp, to whom four pages are devoted.

BOOKS BY ARP

Only recently published works are given here, omitting small brochures of the Dada or surrealist period now out of print.

In the *Age d'Or* series, edited by Henri Parisot for the review *Fontaine,* two volumes: *Le Blanc aux pieds de nègres,* a collection of prose poems, and *Trois nouvelles exemplaires* by Arp and Vicente Huidobro.

Le Siège de l'Air (Ed. Vrille, Paris, 1946). Complete edition of the poems from 1915 to 1945. Dual drawings by Arp and Sophie Taeuber, preface by Alain Gheerbrant.

On my Way (Pub. Wittenborn, New York). Poems and essays by Arp from 1912 to 1947, with the original texts in German and French and their English translation. Essay by Carola Giedion-Welcker. Preface by Robert Motherwell.

Le Voilier dans la forêt (Pub. Louis Broder, October 1957). Contains six original engravings, 14 poems, and 1 poem by Eluard dedicated to Arp.

PRINCIPAL BOOKS AND ARTICLES ON ARP

Michel Seuphor, *Arcadie d'Arp* (La Hune, Paris, 1950). This poem by Seuphor, in a new version, was reproduced in the album *Arp* in the *Prisme* collection (1957), which also contains 45 black and white reproductions of sculptures and reliefs, a short text by Will Grohmann, *Hans Arp, Maler, Plastiker und Poet,* and a bio-bibliographical note in French, English, and German, drawn up by Hans Bolliger. There is also an English translation of Seuphor's prose poem.

Michel Seuphor, *L'art abstrait, ses origines, ses premiers maîtres* (Maeght, Paris, 1949).

Michel Seuphor, *Dictionnaire de la peinture abstraite* (Ed. F. Hazan, Paris, 1957). As well as an article on Arp (pp. 122-123), the part played by Arp and Sophie in the movement is analyzed in the introduction.

André Breton, *Anthologie de l'Humour Noir* (Le Sagittaire, Paris, 1938-1947).

Marcel Jean, *Jalons d'Arp* in *Les Lettres Nouvelles* February 1956.

Herta Wescher, *Le cosmos de Arp* (*Cimaise,* March-April 1957). This remarkable text of about three pages accompanies eleven black and white illustrations.

ILLUSTRATIONS

Since 1916, Arp has illustrated a great number of books of poems, notably those by Richard Huelsenbeck and Tristan Tzara.

DISTINCTIONS

1954: Jean Arp receives the *International Grand Prize for Sculpture at the Venice Biennale,* which may be considered the Nobel Prize of the plastic arts.

1956: With Villon, Brianchon, Chastel, Courthion and Zadkine, a member of the jury for the *Prix de Paris* awarded at the Quadriennale of Rome, under the patronage of the Italian Embassy in France.

He is chosen as a member of the jury of the International Competition of 1957 for a Monument to the Deportees of Auschwitz, but resigns for health reasons.

1957: First Prize in Bronzetto at the Biennale d'Arte Triveneta, Padua.